GET REAL!

Planet Snoz

hahaha   heeheehee

by Phil Kettle

Illustrated by
Melissa Webb

Get Real!
Planet Snoz

Written by Phil Kettle
Illustrations by Melissa Webb
Character design by David Dunstan

Text © 2009 Phil Kettle
Illustrations © 2009 Macmillan Education Australia Pty Ltd

All rights reserved. No part of this publication may be
reproduced, stored in a retrieval system, or transmitted in any
form or by any means, electronic, mechanical, photocopying,
recording, or otherwise, without the prior permission of the
copyright owner. While every care has been taken to trace and
acknowledge copyright, the publishers tender their apologies
for any accidental infringement where copyright has proved
untraceable.

Published by
Macmillan Education Australia Pty Ltd
Level 1, 15–19 Claremont Street, South Yarra,
Victoria 3141
www.macmillan.com.au

Edited by Emma Short

Designed by Jenny Lindstedt,
Goanna Graphics (Vic) Pty Ltd

Printed in China
10 9 8 7 6 5 4 3 2

ISBN: (pack) 9781420278828

ISBN: 9781420276893

Contents

Introduction	5
Chapter One Saturday Morning	7
Chapter Two The Mission	15
Chapter Three The Summons	24
Chapter Four A Devious and Dastardly Plan	31
Chapter Five Training Camp	34
Chapter Six The Big Game	36
Chapter Seven The Plan in Action	43
Chapter Eight Game Time	48
Chapter Nine Victory	56
Let's Write	64
Jesse and Harry Present	66
Word-up!	68
A Laugh a Minute!	70

Introduction

Say hello to Harry Harvard and Jesse Harrison. The one on the right with his eyes closed is Harry. The one on the left who looks like he's just been told that he's won a lifetime supply of potato chips and peanut butter is Jesse. The one that's standing in between Jesse and Harry, looking like she'd rather be somewhere else, is Samantha Smithers.

In fact, the only reason that Sam is standing in between Jesse and Harry is because Harry has promised that he won't talk to her for two months if she has her picture taken with him. And that's the reason Harry's smiling! (The reason Jesse is in the picture is just because he wanted to be.)

Chapter One

Saturday Morning

A NOTE FROM THE AUTHOR

As you already know, most of Harry and Jesse's great adventures begin with them speeding home from Average Primary School. But this adventure begins with Harry and Jesse at home, and that's because it's Saturday morning.

ANOTHER NOTE FROM THE AUTHOR

Actually, if Principal Dorking had his way, all Average Primary School students — except for Jesse and Harry — would be required to attend school on Saturdays to write lines as punishment for their terrible behaviour through the week. So why not Harry and Jesse? Because if you've read another story in this series, **Just Another Day**, you'll know that Principal Dorking had all his bad thoughts about Jesse and Harry removed from his brain by Hugo and Howard from Planet Snoz. Now he thinks that they're the best and brightest boys at Average Primary School! When Principal Dorking saw Mrs Payne in the school corridor, he told her how good he thought Jesse and Harry were. Mrs Payne passed out on the spot!

AVERAGE PRIMARY SCHOOL NEWSLETTER

WRITTEN BY, EDITED BY AND TOTALLY CONTROLLED BY ME — PRINCIPAL DORKING

Dear parents, students, citizens and fans!

It is with great pleasure that I'm able to bring to you another edition of my award-winning newsletter.

You will all be pleased to know that I'm feeling incredibly well considering all the hard work that I do during term-time. My loyal and faithful readers will be especially pleased to know that last week at bowling, I got eight strikes in a row.

IMPORTANT NOTICE

Average Primary School needs to be better than average. It's time for all students to spend an extra day at school each week. Instead of spending Saturdays having fun and playing sport, students should be studying and writing lines at Average Primary School.

Please let me know what you think about this suggestion.

PS: It goes without saying that you are all truly blessed to have me as your principal.

Today, just like every other Saturday, Jesse and Harry were playing soccer for their team, the Golden Boots. The Golden Boots hadn't won a game all year until Jesse and Harry got their time machine. And they hadn't lost a game since then!

The whole town of Average was now a-buzz with the same question.

"Why are the Golden Boots playing like champions, when they used to play like losers?"

"It's like a miracle!" said Samantha Smithers, watching the Golden Boots in their latest match at Average Park. "Jesse and Harry seem to be everywhere on the pitch all at once!"

> **AUTHOR NOTE**
> Of course, we all know why Golden Boots were playing really well and winning all their games.
> TIME MACHINE + JESSE + HARRY =
> VICTORY FOR GOLDEN BOOTS!

And this Saturday, the game proved to be another outstanding and glorious victory for the Golden Boots, just like the last six games. Incredibly, the score was six goals to zero. Jesse and Harry, the stars of the game, scored three fantastic goals each.

6-0! I'll re-start time now...

But this Saturday was also totally different to the last six Saturdays in another way. The last six Saturdays, Jesse and Harry had stayed at the park after the match to sign autographs and have their pictures taken. They also told anyone that wanted to listen (and even those that didn't want to listen) how brilliantly they played.

This Saturday however, Jesse and Harry had no time to waste being soccer stars. They were in a hurry to get back to their tree house. As Jesse and Harry hurriedly left the park, thousands of fans waved and cheered. Harry and Jesse hardly looked back, so they didn't see Samantha Smithers just a few streets behind them. They were on a mission!

Chapter Two

The Mission

The day before yesterday, Jesse and Harry had received an interplanetary text message.

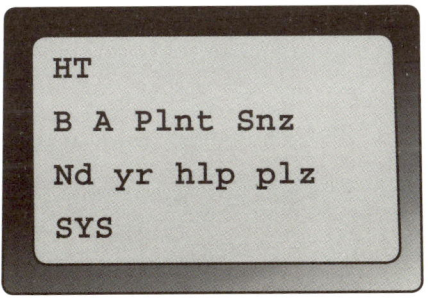

(Translation – Hi there, back at Planet Snoz, need your help please, see you soon!)

A REMINDER FROM THE AUTHOR

Of course, you will all remember how Hugo and Howard, aliens from Planet Snoz, were on their way to the Interplanetary Pick-and-Flick Championship on Planet Pickistan, when they crash-landed their spaceship in the top of the tallest tree in Average Park. And you will also remember that Hugo and Howard were really friendly aliens, but kind of strange looking.

(Well, you should remember if you've read another book in this series, **Just Another Day**!)

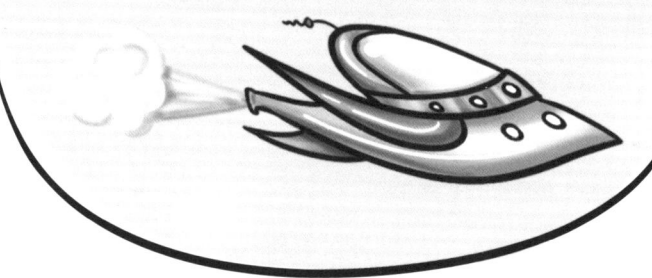

While Jesse and Harry were leading the Golden Boots to yet another outstanding victory, Hugo and Howard were back home on Planet Snoz. They were training with the Planet Snoz soccer team for the Interplanetary Soccer Championship. Teams from all over the universe had entered and Snoz was the host planet. It was always a week of great soccer, great fun and hilarious laughter.

But this year, everything had changed. A spaceship from Planet Dogsbreath had arrived, carrying President Bonsai and the entire Dogsbreath soccer team. President Bonsai had immediately declared that his team had come to win the Interplanetary Soccer Championship. Then he had made two announcements.

All laughter and hilarity are banned for the rest of the tournament. And after the tournament, I am going to take over the entire universe!

When Jesse and Harry got home, they raced to Jesse's mother's kitchen. They needed to stock up on snacks to take with them to Planet Snoz.

Food for the trip to Planet Snoz

- 6 PACKETS OF CHIPS
- 12 CHOCOLATE CHIP COOKIES
- 23 VEGEMITE SANDWICHES
- 10 BANANAS
- 6 ORANGES
- 15 BRUSSELS SPROUTS

The Brussels sprouts weren't for the boys to eat, of course. Jesse wanted to give them to the Snozzie aliens. He was hoping that they might like them enough to come back to Earth and take all the Brussels sprouts in Average back to Planet Snoz.

"Hey, I wonder if Sam likes Brussels sprouts?" Harry asked Jesse.

"Only as much as she likes us," Jesse replied with a laugh. "Maybe we should take Sam with us and leave her on Planet Snoz. I think it might be a really good place for her to live."

Harry and Jesse stuffed their loot into their backpacks and then they were all ready for the big trip.

Jesse picked up the remote control for the time machine and programmed their destination.

Location:
Planet Snoz

Time:
Tomorrow

"Are you ready, Harry?" asked Jesse.

"Of course!" answered Harry.

"Well then, one...*two*...THREE!"

Together, Jesse and Harry put their hands on the red button. And in a blur of dust, a rush of imagination and a whirring of Brussels sprouts, they disappeared into the future.

Chapter Three

The Summons

Quicker than Jesse could eat a packet of chips and a jar of peanut butter in a meteor shower, Jesse and Harry landed on Planet Snoz.

If slimy green aliens who have no sense of humour and don't know how to laugh freak you out a little, then stop reading this story RIGHT NOW!

They found themselves standing right next to Hugo and Howard.

"Harry and Jesse, we're so glad you're here," exclaimed Howard, offering a warm handshake to both boys.

"We need your help again," said Hugo, who was looking a little pale around his eyes.

It didn't take long for Jesse and Harry to learn why Hugo and Howard had summoned them to Planet Snoz.

"President Bonsai from Planet Dogsbreath has brought his soccer team to Snoz to play in the Interplanetary Soccer Championship. He has announced that there is to be no laughter or hilarity for the entire tournament," explained Hugo. "And when the tournament is finished, he is going to take over the entire universe!"

"Aliens from Planet Dogsbreath have no sense of humour at all. But they're really scary," Howard continued. "If they say no one is to laugh, the Interplanetary Soccer Championship will be a very dull and miserable affair. And if President Bonsai takes over the entire universe, then the whole world will become a very dull and miserable affair too!"

Harry and Jesse looked at each other and nodded. Without a moment's hesitation, they agreed to help.

"We're from Average, and we're heroes, and you're our friends, and we love laughter and hilarity!" said Harry.

"So of course we will stay and fight for good times and good jokes," Jesse announced to Snozzie smiles all around.

Hugo and Howard knew that there was no time to waste. They took Jesse and Harry straight to meet their leader, President Poobah. The President was delighted to meet them.

"Average Earthlings, we desperately need your help. Hugo and Howard have told me that you are superheroes."

"Yes," Harry nodded proudly. "Just half an hour ago at home on Earth, we kicked three goals each to lead our team, the Golden Boots, to another magnificent victory on the soccer pitch."

"You'll need to be at your very best to help us defeat the aliens from Dogsbreath," President Poobah replied, looking worried.

"With our superior intellect, we are the tops of our Grade Five class at Average Primary School. And with the help of our

time machine, there isn't a problem in the universe that we can't solve," said Jesse, exaggerating just a little.

"We need to come up with a devious and dastardly plan," said Harry, thinking hard.

Hugo and Howard remembered how devious and dastardly Jesse and Harry were, when they helped extract part of Principal Dorking's brain to make spaceship fuel. They knew that if anyone could come up with a devious and dastardly plan to save the universe from dullness and misery, it would be Jesse Harrison and Harry Harvard.

Chapter Four

A Devious and Dastardly Plan

Of course, it only took a few moments for Jesse and Harry to draw on their incredible ability to create devious and dastardly plans, to create a devious and dastardly plan.

"Planet Snoz will play Planet Dogsbreath in a very serious and non-humorous game of soccer to start the Interplanetary Soccer Championship," Harry announced. "No laughing or hilarity allowed."

President Poobah looked horrified at this suggestion.

"The winner of this match gets to be ruling planet of the universe forever!" Jesse finished.

President Poobah shook his head. He looked concerned. "I don't think that the Snozzies can beat Dogsbreath," he said. "They're a miserable, slimy bunch of players, full of slippery tricks."

Hugo and Howard nodded their heads in agreement.

Approximately twenty-three minutes later, Jesse and Harry had convinced President Poobah that with the help of the two star players of the Golden Boots, Planet Snoz could beat the boring, humourless Dogsbreath team quite easily.

Chapter five

Training Camp

Just as Jesse and Harry were hatching their devious and dastardly plan, President Bonsai of Dogsbreath was leading his team in a training session at Lunar Park.

"When we win this tournament," announced President Bonsai, "I will declare that Planet Dogsbreath rules the universe. I will be the greatest leader the universe has ever seen."

Suddenly, President Bonsai's mobile phone beeped. It was a text message from President Poobah.

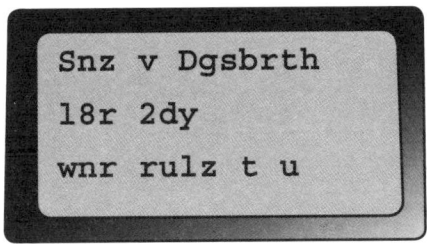

(Translation – Snoz versus Dogsbreath, later today, winner rules the universe.)

Then President Poobah received a reply.

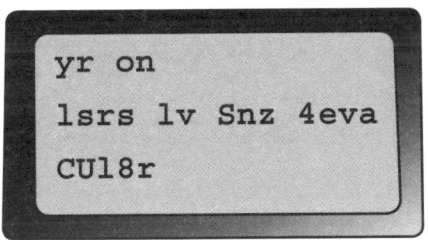

(Translation – you're on, losers leave Snoz forever, see you later)

"Awesome!" said Jesse. "Now all we have to do is win."

"Let's get to work," said Harry.

Chapter Six

The Big Game

Within minutes, the news of the opening match of the Interplanetary Soccer Championship had spread. Spaceships from all over the universe started to arrive in the parking lot of Snoz Stadium. The whole of Planet Snoz was buzzing with excitement and expectation. President Poobah arrived at the stadium to address the crowd.

"Citizens of our great planet, I'm pleased to announce that our fabulous and fantastic Snoz soccer team is going to play the miserable slimy team from Planet Dogsbreath in the first match of the Interplanetary Soccer Championship. If we lose, then Planet Dogsbreath will become ruling planet of the universe. And that would be really bad because no one in the universe will be able to laugh or have fun ever again."

Planet Snoz

"But, my fellow Snozzies," the President continued. "I do have some good news. We have recruited Average Earthlings, Jesse Harrison and Harry Harvard, to lead our team to victory. They may come from Average, but they are a lot better than average!"

While President Poobah addressed the crowd at Snoz Stadium, Jesse and Harry made a list of everything they would need from their tree house to help put their devious and dastardly plan into action.

Stuff for our plan

2 CANS OF ANTI-SLIME SPRAY

2 PACKETS OF PEPPER

2 PACKETS OF ITCHY POWDER

JESSE'S SOCCER BOOTS

HARRY'S SOCCER BOOTS

Jesse programmed their destination into the time machine. Together they pressed the blue button to de-activate the time machine and return them to now time.

A millisecond later, Harry and Jesse were back in their tree house. They were rifling through their wooden chest, stuffing their backpacks with everything they had written on the list, when suddenly they heard a sneeze.

"Did you hear that, Harry?" asked Jesse.

"Sure did," said Harry.

"SAM!" they shouted together.

"Hi!" called Sam from beneath the tree house. "What are you doing?"

"We're just heading off to Planet Snoz to play in an interplanetary soccer tournament," said Jesse, looking out of the tree house window.

"Yeah, right!" laughed Sam.

Then Jesse re-programmed their original destination and together the boys pressed the red button that would take them back to Snoz.

Chapter Seven

The Plan in Action

The boys arrived back in the Snoz team's dressing room at Snoz Stadium.

"It's time to put our devious and dastardly plan into action," said Jesse.

It took Jesse and Harry seven minutes and thirty-two seconds to explain it to the Snoz team.

"So, what do you think?" Harry asked.

There was a moment of total silence. Then…

While President Poobah, Hugo, Howard and the rest of the Snozzies were rolling around laughing, Jesse and Harry snuck into the Dogsbreath team's dressing room.

The Dogsbreath players were so busy preparing for the game, they didn't see Harry and Jesse sneak into their room. And they definitely didn't see them sprinkling itchy powder into their boots and jumpers.

Back in the Snoz dressing room, Harry and Jesse changed into their soccer boots and shirts. Then both of them grabbed a packet of pepper and stuffed it into their socks.

Finally, they reached into their backpacks and pulled out thirteen cans of anti-slime spray. They started handing them around to their Snozzie teammates.

"Here," said Harry. "Put these cans of anti-slime spray in your noses. When you get close to a Dogsbreath player, give him a quick spray!"

"Those Dogsbreath players will just melt away," laughed Jesse.

"Oh, you two are both so devious and mischievous," said Hugo with a smile.

Chapter eight

Game Time

The crowd was roaring. They were really excited, but really scared at the same time. Some of the Snozzies in the crowd were desperately cracking joke after joke and laughing uncontrollably. They knew that if Dogsbreath beat Snoz, then laughter would be banned forever.

The Snoz players ran out onto the pitch. With only a minute to go before the start of the game, Jesse and Harry called the players into a huddle. Together they watched the Dogsbreath team run out onto the pitch.

Suddenly the Dogsbreath players started scratching. Then they started rolling on the ground and moaning. Then there was more scratching, then more rolling, then more scratching – and then lots of yelling.

"It looks like our plan is working," Harry told the rest of the Snoz team. "Anyway, this is the most important game in the history of the universe and I only have *one* thing to say…don't forget the three Ps!"

"That'd be *three* things to say then," said Jesse.

"OK, I only have *three* things to say," Harry frowned.

And with that, the referee blew the whistle to start the game. Harry and Jesse took off at a run, sprinkling pepper all over the pitch.

Back in the centre of the ground, the Snozzies started to breathe in the pepper and then they started to sneeze.

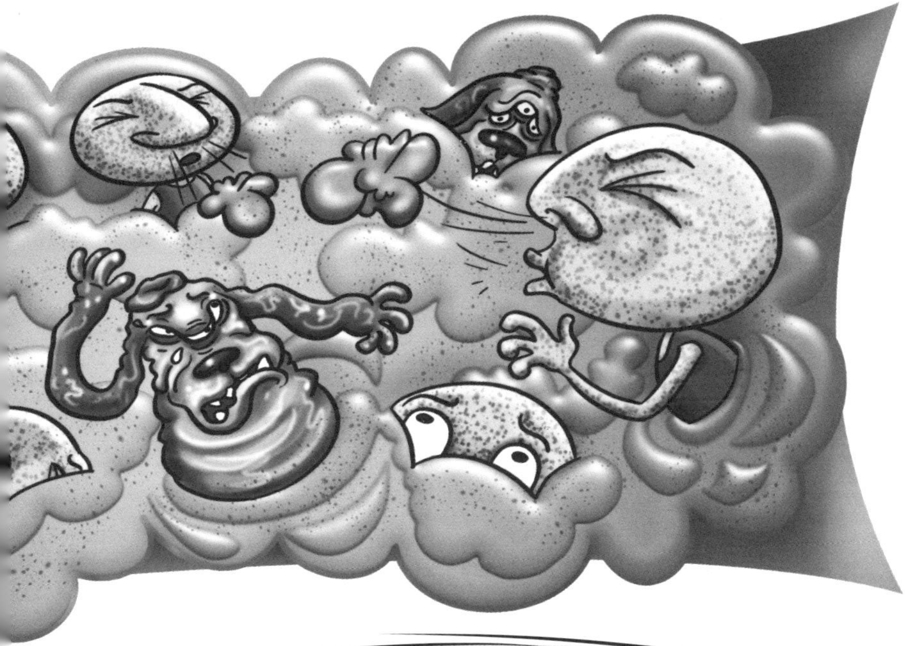

AUTHOR NOTE
When you've got a nose as big as an alien from Snoz, a sneeze is not just a normal sneeze!

The first sneezes were so powerful that soon the entire stadium was filled with flying pepper. Then even the crowd started sneezing, sending giant globs of green goo flying right across the stadium.

SNOZ STADIUM

Snoz	400
Dogsbreath	0

While the Dogsbreath team was rolling and scratching and moaning and yelling, the Snoz team was sneezing giant globs of green goo across the pitch. Jesse and Harry grabbed the ball. With their tiny Earth-size noses, the flying pepper had not affected them, so they managed to score about two hundred goals each!

President Bonsai was furious. He ran into the middle of the ground to try and stop the game. Just then, the sneezing Snozzies reached into their socks and pulled out their anti-slime spray. Soon President Bonsai was nothing more than a small puddle of angry slime on the grass.

Chapter Nine

Victory

By the time the final siren blew, Jesse and Harry had scored another two hundred goals each. Planet Snoz had won the right to be the ruling planet of the universe. The whole of Snoz Stadium went wild!

"Harry and Jesse," said President Poobah. "I hereby award you the electronic keycard to Planet Snoz!"

There was nothing left for the Average superheroes to do, but wave goodbye to Hugo and Howard, then whiz through time and space back to their tree house…

A REMINDER FROM THE AUTHOR

Of course, as we all know, when the time machine transports Harry and Jesse away to another adventure, time stands still in Average. So for Sam, no time had passed at all.

"And I'm the queen of England!"

"What?" said Jesse.

"Huh?" said Harry.

"I said 'yeah, right, and I'm the queen of England!'" Sam repeated.

"Oh, are you still here?" asked Jesse, looking out of the tree house window.

"Not for long," said Sam. And she wandered off, still laughing quietly to herself.

AUTHOR WARNING

The bad news for Jesse and Harry was that back on Earth, and more specifically, in Average, the part of Principal Dorking's brain that had been removed was **growing back**. And so were those bad thoughts about Harry and Jesse...

Let's Write

Planning the Destination

We've already covered story ideas and creating a plan with a location and characters. We've also practised creating powerful introductions. Now we need to come up with a good ending.

You might think that it's a bit soon to be planning the ending, or as I like to refer to it, the destination. But the reason that I like to plan the destination early is that I like to have something to aim for – or a direction that I want my story to take.

For example, if I was writing a story about football, I might aim to have the story finish with my team playing in the grand final, winning the premiership and me winning the 'best on ground' award! So open up your creative-writing book and on the top of a new page, write:

My story plan – destination

A destination is something that you aim for, but it might change while you are writing your story. For example, in my story about football, I might decide to change the destination – I was tackled, broke my leg at the very start of the game and ended up in hospital.

Practise writing some destinations for your story ideas. And remember, a destination is something to aim for but your story might not get there, or the destination might change along the way.

Jesse and Harry Present

About the Author

Jesse: *Hey Phil, I think I know where you got the idea for this story.*

Phil: *And where would that be?*

Jesse: *Simple. The end of* Just Another Day *was also the start for this story.*

Phil: *Gee Jesse, it's no wonder you're the top of Grade Five at Average Primary School.*

Jesse: *Is writing a series a lot of fun?*

Phil: *It sure is. With each story I write, I get to find out more about the characters. For example, I know a lot more about you now than I did when I wrote the* The Time Machine. *By the way Jesse, how does poor Mrs Payne put up with you and Harry?*

Jesse: *Easy! We're really good!*

Phil: *Ummmmh!*

About the Illustrator

Harry: Hey Melissa, how do you get humour into your illustrations?

Melissa: Usually I just start drawing and ideas pop into my head.

Harry: Where would you most like to live – Planet Snoz or Planet Dogsbreath?

Melissa: It sometimes feels like both at my house.

Harry: I know the feeling!

hahahee teehee
heeheehee hohoho

Word-up!

Full name: what your parents call you when they're angry with you

Fable: the story you tell your parents when you've done something wrong

Grandparents: the people that think you're great even when your parents don't

Gum: glue for hair

Heroes: what a guy in a boat does (He-rows!)

Top bunk: where you should never put someone who wets the bed

Toothache: the pain that drives you to extraction

Smile: a curve that can set a lot of things straight

A Laugh a Minute!

What do elves learn in school?
The elf-abet!

What holds the sun up in the sky?
Sunbeams!

What did the pencil sharpener say to the pencil?
Stop going in circles and get to the point!

How does the barber cut the moon's hair?
E-clipse it!

What happened when the wheel was invented?
It caused a revolution!

What kind of plates do they use on Mars?
Flying saucers!

Other Titles in the Series

The Time Machine

Ferret Attack

The Trouble with...

Just Another Day

Big City Museum

The Flying Machines

Snooping Snoopalot

The Pirate Play

The Last Day

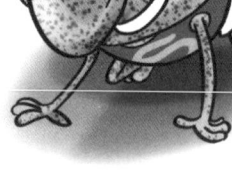